CLASSIC
GUITAR DUETS

Arranged by Leonid Bolotine

3603

MUSIC MINUS ONE GUITAR

Andrew LaFreniere, *1st Guitar*
Ernest Bracco, *2nd Guitar*

CLASSIC
GUITAR DUETS

Arranged by Leonid Bolotine

3603

PAVANA

3 taps (1 measure) precede music.

Grave, maestoso (M.M. ♩ = 54)

Luis Milan, the famous Spanish lutenist of the XVI century composed this Pavana as a solo lute piece. The Pavana was a stately court dance of the period and this is one of the better known.

GAGLIARDA

3 taps (1 measure) precede music.

Allegro moderato (M.M. ♩ = 84)

Vincenzo Galilei was the father of the great astronomer, Galileo, and was in his own right a celebrated lutenist of the XVI century. He composed a great number of works for the lute, among them this Gagliarda, one of the loveliest to reach our times.

4

INVENTION

4 taps + 2 silent beats (1-½ measures)
precede music.

The Invention by the great Bach is one of a series which he composed for the keyboard. Although this is a popular student piece, it still reveals his genius as the great master of the fugue.

Moderato

MENUET

3 taps (1 measure)
precede music.

This Menuet is from the notebook of Anna Magdalena Bach for which Bach
composed. It was also originally a keyboard piece.

J. S. BACH

(M.M. ♩ = 72)

MINUET
from "Don Giovanni"

This Minuetto is from Mozart's immortal opera, "Don Giovanni' and is heard
near the end of the first act.

3 taps (1 measure)
precede music.

(M.M. ♩ = 66)

SPRING SONG

Although the Spring Song has been performed an infinite number of times, it still remains one of the loveliest and finest examples of XIX century poetic romanticism.

Allegretto grazioso (M.M. ♩ = 63)

MINUET

5 taps (1-⅔ measures) + 1 silent beat
precede music.

This celebrated Menuet by Beethoven earned the sub-title of "The Menuet in
G" but it was not so named by the composer. This particular arrangement was
transposed to the key of C for reasons of simplification.

Moderately (M.M. ♩ =72)

PRELUDE No. 1

The genius of Chopin is too well known to add anything new. The first prelude, although written originally for the piano lends itself admirably to this combination of two guitars.

4 taps (1 measure) precede music.

Largo (M.M. ♩ = 48)

PRELUDE No. 2

This prelude, although lighter in mood than the first, is also an excellent piece for guitar duet.

5 taps (1-⅔ measures) precede music.

Andantino (M.M. ♩ = 66)

ETUDE

This immortal melody is from Chopin's Etude No. 3 for the piano. Although the player will be required to reach for high notes, he may benefit in two ways. First, he will get acquainted with this seldom used register, second, he will be rewarded by the beauty of these notes.

3 taps (1-½ measures) + 1 silent beat
precede music.

AIR

from "The Pearl Fishers"

This aria was one for which the great Caruso was noted and for which he
received much acclaim.

BARCAROLLE
from "The Tales of Hoffman"

The Barcarole from Offenbach's opera, "The Tales of Hoffman" is still one
of the great favorites throughout the world.

Moderato (M.M. ♩. = 50)

ETUDE in A Major

Matteo Carcassi was a famous Italian guitarist of the mid XIX century.
Although this etude was composed for guitar solo, the second part does much to
add a certain charm.

4 taps (1 measure)
precede music.

Andantino (M.M. ♩ =72)

14

ROMANCE ANTIGUO

5 taps (1-2/3 measures) + 1 silent beat
precede music.

This piece by an anonymous (probably Spanish) composer is more popular
today than it was at the time of its creation.

LA PALOMA

Allegretto

2 taps (1 measure)
precede music.

This famous Mexican folk tune hardly needs an introduction. The player
should know his part well before attempting to play it with the second guitar.

MUSIC MINUS ONE GUITAR CLASSICS

CHAMBER CLASSICS

BOCCHERINI Guitar Quintet No. 4 in D 'Fandango' MMO CD 3601
Andrew Keeping, guitar - Da Vinci Quartet

CASTELNUOVO-TEDESCO Sonatina;
GIULIANI Serenata, op. 127 MMO CD 3622
Christian Reichert, guitar - Katarzyna Bury, flute

Classic Guitar Duets MMO CD 3603
Andrew LaFreniere, 1st guitar - Ernest Bracco, 2nd guitar
Anonymous (arr. Bolotine) *Romance Antigui; J.S. Bach* (arr. Bolotine) *Invention; Notebook of Anna Magdalena Bach: Menuet;* Beethoven (arr. Bolotine) *Minuet in C major (transposed from 'Minuet in G');* Bizet (arr. Bolotine) *Les Pêcheurs de Perles: Air;* Carcassi (arr. Bolotine) *Etude in A major;* Chopin (arr. Bolotine) *Prelude, op. 28, no. 20; Prelude, op. 28, no. 7; Etude, op. 10, no. 3 (Lento, ma non troppo);* Galilei, Vincenzo (arr. Bolotine) *Gagliarda;* Mendelssohn (arr. Bolotine) *Spring Song;* Milán (arr. Bolotine) *Pavana;* Mozart (arr. Bolotine) *Don Giovanni, KV527 - Act I: Minuetto;* Offenbach (arr. Bolotine) *Les Contes d'Hoffmann (Tales of Hoffman): Barcarolle (Moderato);* Trad. (arr. Bolotine) *La Paloma*

Classical & Romantic Guitar Duets MMO CD 3605
Edward Flower, 1st guitar - David McLellan, 2nd guitar
Albéniz (arr. Flower) *Malagueña;* Anckermann (arr. Flower) *El Arroyo que Murmura;* Carulli *Duet in F major: Rondo (Allegretto); Duo in E major: Largo; Allegretto; Study in A major: Andante;* Fauré *Pelleas et Melisande - Sicilienne: Allegretto molto moderato;* Granados (arr. Flower) *Spanish Dances, op. 37, H142: 2. Orièntale; 5. Andaluza (Playera);* Scheidler *Sonata in D major: Romanze;* Sor *Andantino; Marche; Duo in A major: Andante; Allegretto*

GIULIANI Guitar Quintet in A major, op. 65 MMO CD 3602
Andrew Keeping, guitar - The DaVinci Quartet: Catherine Morgan, 1st violin; Joshua Fisher, 2nd violin; Juliette Jopling, viola; Andrew Skrimshire

Guitar and Flute Duets, vol. I MMO CD 3606
Edward Flower, guitar - Jeremy Barlow, flute
Anonymous *Green Sleeves to a Ground; Faronell's Ground; J.S. Bach Sonata in C major, BWV1033; E.G. Baron Sonata in G major; Couperin Sœur Monique; Dowland If My Complaints; Finger Division on a Ground; Pilkington Rest Sweet Nymphs; Vivaldi Andante (arranged from the Flute Concerto in G major, RV438)*

Guitar and Flute Duets, vol. II MMO CD 3607
Edward Flower, guitar - Jeremy Barlow, flute
Fauré *Pelleas et Melisande: Sicilienne;* Giuliani *Grand Duo Concertant (Sonata) for Flute and Guitar, op. 85;* Ibert *Entr'acte;* Schubert *An die Musik, op. 88, no. 4, D547;* Villa-Lobos *Bachianas Brasileiras No. 5; Distribution of the Flowers (Distribucao de Flores)*

PIAZZOLLA Histoire du Tango and other Latin Classics for Guitar & Flute Duet MMO CD 3619
Christian Reichert, guitar - Katarzyna Bury, flute
Granados (arr. Reichert & Bury) *Spanish Dances, op. 37, H142: 5. Andaluza (Playera);* Piazzolla *Histoire du Tango: 1. Bordel 1900; 2. Café; 3. Nightclub; 4. Concert d'aujourd'hui;* Sarasate *Romanza Andaluza; Playera*

Renaissance & Baroque Guitar Duets MMO CD 3604
Edward Flower, 1st guitar - David McLellan, 2nd guitar
Anonymous *La Rossignol; Drewries' Accordes; My Lady Carey's Dompe; Lesson;* C.P.E. Bach *Marche; Polonaise;* J.S. Bach *Musette in D major, BWV Anh. 126; Menuet; Prelude; Fugue; Invention;* Dowland *My Lord Chamberlain's Galliard; Tarleton's Resurrection; My Lord Willoughby's Welcome Home;* J. Johnson *The Flatt Pavin;* Lawes *Suite: I. Corant I; II. Alman; III. Corant II;* Pilkington *Echo;* Richee *Echo;* Telemann *Canon;* Trad. (English folk song) *Greensleeves*

FERNANDO SOR *Classic guitar duos - Intermediate level* MMO CD 3633
Christian Reichert, primo guitar; Beata Będkowska-Huang, secondo guitar
Divertissement, op. 38; L'Encouragement: Fantaisie pour deux Guitarres, op. 34; Souvenir de Russie, op. 63

INSTRUMENTAL CLASSICS WITH ORCHESTRA

CASTELNUOVO-TEDESCO Concerto No. 1 in D major, op. 99 MMO CD 3618
Christian Reichert, guitar - Plovdiv Philharmonic Orchestra/Nayden Todorov

GIULIANI Concerto No. 1 in A major, op. 30 MMO CD 3617
Christian Reichert, guitar - Plovdiv Philharmonic Orchestra/Nayden Todorov

Orchestral Gems for Classical Guitar MMO CD 3615
Andrew LaFreniere, guitar - Stuttgart Festival Orchestra/Emil Kahn
Bizet *L'Arlesienne Suite: III. Adagietto;* Foster *Old Folks at Home;* Gruber (m) Mohr (l) *Silent Night (arranged for soloist with orchestral accompaniment);* Lehár *Die Lustige Witwe (The Merry Widow): 'Vilja';* Offenbach *Les Contes d'Hoffmann (Tales of Hoffman): Barcarolle (Moderato);* Rimsky-Korsakov *Song of India;* Tchaikovsky *Chanson Triste;* Trad. *Drink to Me Only with Thine Eyes;* Yradier (Iradier) *La Paloma*

RODRIGO Concierto de Aranjuez MMO CD 3616
Christian Reichert, guitar - Plovdiv Philharmonic Orchestra/Nayden Todorov

RODRIGO Fantasia para un Gentilhombre MMO CD 3621
Christian Reichert, guitar - Plovdiv Philharmonic Orchestra/Nayden Todorov

VIVALDI Two Concerti for Guitar (Lute) & Orchestra
C major, RV425; D major, RV93 MMO CD 3623
Christian Reichert - Taunus String Orchestra

LATIN CLASSICS

Baden-Powell Revisited
Brazilian Love Songs for Guitar & Rhythm Section MMO CD 3628
Christian Reichert, guitar
Baden Powell *Chará; Samba de Pintinho; Quaquaraquaquá; Fim de Linha; Valse No. 1; Samba Triste; Tempo Feliz; Cidade Vazia; Babel; Casa Velha*

POP, BLUES & JAZZ CLASSICS

Cool Jazz for Guitar MMO CD 3620
Tony DePaolo, guitar - The MMO Band
You Gotta Be; Sweetest Taboo; Let it Flow; Been So Long; No Ordinary Love; Unbreak My Heart; All around the World; Another Sad Love Song

For Guitarists Only! *Jimmy Raney Small Band Arrangements* MMO CD 3612
Jack Wilkins, 1st guitar - Jimmy Raney, 2nd guitar; Stan Getz, tenor saxophone; Hal McCusick, clarinet/flute; George Duvivier, bass; Ed Shaughnessy, drums: A master class in jazz technique—Jack Wilkins demonstrates!
Fools Rush In; I've Got It Bad and That Ain't Good; Just You, Just Me; How About You?; Sunday; Beta Minus; Jupiter; Spring Is Here; Darn that Dream; This Heart of Mine

Play The Blues Guitar *A Dick Weissman Method* MMO CD 3614
Dick Weissman, guitar: Blues master Dick Weissman explains and demonstrates guitar techniques (strums, chords, picking, alternate tunings, etc.) with some great blues classics, such as "Frankie and Johnny" and "Kansas City Blues." Mr. Weissman demonstrates, provides accompaniments and guides you through. At the end of this master class you'll be calling yourself a blues pro!

Ten Duets for Two Guitars *Play Either Part!* MMO CD 3613
George Barnes, 1st guitar - Carl Kress, 2nd guitar
All I Do Is Dream of You; My Blue Heaven; Don't Get Around Much Anymore; Stompin' at the Savoy; Swingin' Down the Lane; Stairway to the Stars; I'm Thru with Love; Alice Blue Gown; Londonderry Air; Try a Little Tenderness

STUDENT SERIES

Bluegrass Guitar MMO CD 3608
Russ Barenberg, guitar - Country Cooking Bluegrass Band: Peter Wernick, banjo & vocals; John Miller, bass & vocals; Greg Root, mandolin; Kenny Kossek, fiddle; Nondi Leonard, vocals: Develop basic bluegrass techniques, based on the styles of groups such as Bill Monroe and the Blue Grass Boys, Flatt and Scruggs, Foggy Mountain Boys. The Stanley Brothers and the Clinch Mountain Boys. The guitar solos on the CD are written out note-for-note in easy-to-follow tablature notation in the enclosed booklet.
The Ballad of Jed Clampett; Foggy Mountain Breakdown; It's in My Mind to Ramble; Salty Dog Blues; Dark Hollow; Late Last Night; Dueling Banjo; Mountain Dew; Lonesome Road Blues; Little Maggie; Roll on Buddy; Sitting on Top of the World; Jesse James; All the Good Times Are Past and Gone

Favorite Folks Songs For Guitar MMO CD 3611
Harry Tuft, guitar - Dick Weissman, guitar; Judy Roderick, vocals: More than just a collection of folk songs, Harry Tuft and Dick Weissman have created an album designed to aid the beginning guitarist in everything from holding the guitar properly to illustrating a large selection of strums and chords along with each song. A complete method for the beginner, illustrated with finger positions and fret diagrams as well as notation for each song.
Hush Little Baby; Oh, Mary Don't You Weep; I Know Where I'm Going; East Virginia; The Cuckoo; Cool Colorado; Five Hundred Miles; Spanish Is the Loving Tongue; The Sloop 'John B'; Key to the Highway; Stackolee; Silver Dagger; Man of Constant Sorrow; Walking Boss; This Train; He's Got the Whole World in His Hands; Down in the Valley; Banks of the Ohio; Greensleeves

How To Play the Folk Guitar MMO CD 3610
Dick Weissman, banjo - Dan Fox, guitar: This thorough introduction to the magic of the folk guitar will help you develop basic and more advanced techniques: strums, arpeggios, calypso strums, finger picks, duet playing, upper forms of the common chords, and more, along with a wonderful selection of great folk classics.

Play the Guitar *Easy Way to Learn Chords and Rhythms,*
by George Barnes & Bob Mersey MMO CD 3609
George Barnes, guitar - Bob Mersey, narration: A complete introduction to popular guitar playing, from basic chords, triplets, downstrokes, sonata accompaniment, through different rhythmic variations: cha-cha, New Orleans, shuffle, blues, Nashville, country, and many more. Truly the easiest way to become an expert in the full range of popular guitar stylings.

MUSIC MINUS ONE
50 Executive Boulevard
Elmsford, New York 10523-1325
1.800.669.7464 (U.S.)/914.592.1188 (International)

www.musicminusone.com | e-mail: mmogroup@musicminusone.com

MMO 3603   Pub. No. 00157